How to Turn Generation Me Into Active Members of Your Association

---

By Cynthia D'Amour

Jump Start Books
Ann Arbor, MI

How to Turn Generation Me Into Active Members of Your Association

By Cynthia D'Amour

Jump Start Books
Ann Arbor, MI

How to Turn Generation Me Into Active Members of Your Association

*This book is dedicated
to Mom and Dad,
for being great parents
who got me involved in clubs early in life,
and to my husband James,
for being my best friend.
Thank you!*

ISBN 0-9654600-1-0

To order additional copies of this book,
simply call, toll free:
1-888-994-3375

Table of Contents

Acknowledgments

A book is not produced by the author alone. It takes long hours of input and work from many people.

I would like to take a moment to thank the following people for helping me:

To all of the organizations that I belonged to and boards that I served through the years. My experiences with you taught me the powerful lessons that I am sharing in this book.

To all of the people who helped to review my rough drafts. Your feedback kept me on track.

To my friend **Kay Seidel**. Thank you for believing in my capabilities — and reminding me when I forgot.

To my friend **Gerry Romano**. Thank you for opening up the world of writing for associations for me.

To **Fred and Carol Model**. Thank you for a stimulating Thanksgiving dinner that started the wheels turning.

And finally, to **my family and my husband James**. This book exists because of your constant and loving support. Thank you.

Welcome to "Generation Me"

There's a rumor out there that the "Me Generation" does not want to get involved in your association and chapter activities.

Have you heard it? Are you experiencing it?

If I've heard it once, I've heard it a hundred times all over the country from chapter leaders — like you.

The interesting thing is, the "Me Generation" has been described as Generation X, people in their 30's and 40's, those "flower children that never grew up," and every age in between.

The descriptions of the "Me Generation" varies by city, industry and type of association.

What they all have in common, is that they are people who "should" belong to your associations, — but aren't joining because they're "too busy with life."

I'm going to rename them, "Generation Me" — it's the secret to turning them into active members...

Generation Me is not defined by age.

They are a new group of potential active members who
need to be sold over and over on why they should
invest their time being involved in your association and
chapter activities.

**The value of their time determines their potential
involvement in your chapter.**

Let's look at the typical life of Generation Me.

They live in a stressed out, time poverty era.
Technology keeps advancing — creating more to learn
and constant change.

In many homes, it takes two incomes to make ends
meet. Work life is demanding. Down-sizing, right-
sizing, and mergers are abundant — creating chaos and
extra work.

Their children have soccer games, music lessons and
schedules as tight as many adults.

Generation Me takes time to workout to stay healthy —
and needs some time to relax and sleep!

On top of all of this, is your chapter meeting!

**Demands on time are the real competition you face to
get people active in your chapter.**

At this point, you may be frustrated. Their life sounds
like yours — and, you've made time for your chapter!

Why can't they?

"Generation Me is a bunch of lazy and selfish people," you may insist!

From where you're sitting, I can see your point of view. You may even think recruiting Generation Me is a hopeless waste of time.

It doesn't have to be this way...

Generation Me CAN be turned into active members of your association and chapter — it's just going to take a change in perspective, some marketing savvy and a few polished skills.

I've written this book as a road map to help you successfully transform Generation Me into active members — and perhaps future leaders.

It's based on my experience of more than 30 total years of serving on boards and recruiting more than 250 members to the various associations that I belonged to — and my experiences with the groups I left.

I was born in the years that the generations shifted gears from Baby Boomer to Generation X.

Although I grew up with a lot of Baby Boomer training, I don't remember the day Kennedy died.

In fact, as I hit my 30's I pulled away from my Boomer life and seemed to join Gen X as they hit their stride.

What does this have to do with you?

Since I developed these strategies with experience in both generations, they will work with whatever group you define as Generation Me.

It's going to be up to you to test these strategies and customize them to your chapter.

If you're up to the challenge, I'm ready to teach you how to turn Generation Me into active members of your association and chapter.

Let's get going! It's time to start with the basics...

— Chapter One —

Basics for Working With Generation Me

Before we get into detailed strategies, we need to lay a foundation of some basic concepts about working with Generation Me to insure your success in turning them into active members.

A Public Attitude Adjustment

Start believing that Generation Me can and will become active members of your association.

Get rid of any attitudes or anger towards Generation Me's current lack of participation.

People can pick up it up a mile away if you do not like them — or expect little from them.

As a leader, you set the pace for your chapter.

Your new belief will inspire hope in your current members and help open the doors to new ideas about how to reach Generation Me.

3 Reasons Why Generation Me Gets Involved

There are three major reasons why people will get involved in your association and chapter.

1. Professional/Personal Development

We live in an era that demands lifelong learning in order to keep up with all the changes.

• How can you improve the quality of their life or make their job easier?

• What skills and knowledge can they learn or improve by being involved?

• Will being active in your chapter help them advance in their career?

2. Contribution to a "Greater Good"

Whether you are a professional, trade, civic or fraternal group, many of your potential members are motivated by helping some greater good.

It may take form in student involvement, mentoring, scholarships, collecting for the needy, some form of community involvement, etc.

The possibilities are endless — and need to be relevant to your members.

3. Belonging to a "Community"

People want to be able to network, have fun, and build quality relationships that fulfill personal and professional needs.

They want to feel like they belong.

You need to support them in their goals and make sure your members have lots of opportunity to bond with each other.

These three reasons create the return for the time people invest in your association and chapter.

Helping people realize the value your chapter offers takes savvy marketing. We'll get into specific, how-to strategies for you to use in the next chapter.

Your Defining Statement

From here on in this book, we're going to talk from a chapter perspective.

Chapters interact most personally with members — and, thus, need to be the best marketers.

If you're at a national level, all of the strategies discussed will still apply — you'll just need to think of them in broader terms.

Strong chapters fuel strong national organizations.

We are also going to refer to "Generation Me" as your members from now on.

Generation Me is a group of members who will pay their dues and become very active when they see that being involved is the best use of their time.

Dropping the "us" versus "them" mentality will also help you to project your chapter as a warm and welcoming group.

With that housekeeping done, let's get back to creating a defining statement for your chapter...

• **You need to know who you are, before you can start filling potential member needs.**

That is, you need to define the niche your chapter fills in our world — your unique selling position that describes the very essence of who you are.

Once you identify your defining statement, you will incorporate it into everything about your chapter — from how you sell it to how you run it.

• **Discovering your defining statement is a process.**

I went through this process with a women business owners group. Our obvious niche was women business owners — but, this was not enough.

Women business owners are a huge and diverse group of people. We needed to narrow our focus.

First, we turned to our most active members and asked why they were involved.

Next, we explored what other organizations and services worked with women business owners — to see how we were different from them.

We discovered that most groups served established business owners. Our members tended to be fairly new one-person operations and home-based.

Our meetings also created a safe environment to explore being a business owner.

We decided to define our group as an organization for baby businesses and women who were "pregnant" with a business idea and wanted to explore.

Previously, the group had been floundering. With our defining statement as our driving concept, we went on to quadruple our membership in two years.

It's powerful stuff when you get the right statement!

So, what is your chapter about? Who do you serve? What slice of the market do you specialize in?

• **Four more tips about defining statements.**

1. Your defining statement needs to be something your members can identify with.

"Baby business" and "pregnant with an idea" is not the most sophisticated language. Yet, when people heard it, if it was right for them, they felt like they had found their "home" — and quickly became loyal members.

2. The words need to mean something.

This is going to be the driving marketing force for your chapter. Meaningless words get meaningless results.

3. Try to paint a picture with your defining statement.

Help people visualize if they or someone they may know will benefit from being involved in your group.

Word pictures, such as "baby businesses," also help people remember your chapter so they can make appropriate referrals to potential members.

4. Be specific — niches can even vary by chapter.

This is especially true when there are many chapters in the same geographic area. You need to create your niche so people know where your chapter fits best.

Are you the social or professionally serious group? Focused on starting careers or maturing careers? Lots of one industry or mixed membership?

There are no "right" answers. The key is that your defining statement reflects who you are as a chapter — in other words, your target market for membership.

Now that you've got your basics, let's start marketing to your members...

— Chapter Two —

How to Market to Your Members

The Continual Sale

Because of the increased competition for their time, your members are constantly reevaluating whether or not your chapter is a worthy investment for them.

This is nothing personal. Constant demand on time is a reality. So are too many options.

Help your members make staying involved in your chapter an easy decision by incorporating savvy marketing into everything you do.

How to Hit Your Members' Hot Buttons

Every time you ask your members for a chunk of their time, whether to do committee work or to attend a meeting, a sale takes place.

You are selling an opportunity for their time.

11

You need WIIFM — what's in it for me?

Your members will make time for that which is important to them. When you ask for their time, make sure you include what they will get out of it — hit their hot buttons with WIIFM.

Hot buttons are those little switches in our head that say this is a good opportunity for ME!

Your members' hot buttons reflect the reasons that they joined your chapter— professional development, contributing to greater good or that sense of belonging.

WIIFM and hitting hot buttons is a must for announcements as well as written materials.

For example, "We need people to sell raffle tickets prior to the meeting," is very self-centered — focusing only on chapter needs.

Why should your member help you out?

"We have a great opportunity for someone to sell raffle tickets at our next meeting. You'll have an excuse to start a conversation with anyone. You'll also help send a special student to college this year with the money you collect."

Now you have painted a very different picture. Your member gets help with networking and contributes to a student's education by helping.

You've just hit two possible hot buttons.

The more WIIFM you include in everything you do, the more active your members will be.

Features, Benefits and Solutions

When you are creating WIIFM statements, you want to think in terms of features, benefits, and solutions.

Features are statements of fact.

Benefits are results provided by features.

Solutions help address a bigger picture.

Using our raffle ticket example...

Feature: Selling tickets

Benefits: Networking opportunity
Fundraising for chapter

Solutions: Easier talking to people
Sending special student to school

Here's another example for attending meetings...

Feature: 50+ people attend each meeting

Benefit: Great networking opportunity

Solutions: Learn from industry professionals
Resources and solutions
Leads to your next job
Make new friends

Solutions make things personal — and hit people's hot buttons better.

When you turn features into benefits and solutions, keep your members' needs in mind — they might not be the same as yours.

For example, you may see 50 people attending in terms of more potential volunteers to recruit. Your member may see "opportunity to get recruited for committee work" as a reason to stay home!

Use different benefits and solutions to attract different segments of your membership.

Customize when you can. If not, give a variety appropriate for the people you want to persuade.

7 Tips for Hitting Hot Buttons in Your Written Materials

1. Start by brainstorming with your members in mind.

Keep in mind, sometimes the best solutions come last.

2. How many benefits and solutions to use?

- Minimum to list is three.

- Most people can't handle more than five under one heading.

- Always have an odd number listed.

3. Order to use: Strong - Weak - Second Strongest.

Once you've selected the best benefits and solutions to use, decide which one is your absolutely strongest, most persuasive, hot button hitting item. When making your list, lead with it.

The "weakest" of this group goes in the middle. List your second strongest benefit last so you end on a powerful note.

4. Your headline can make or break you.

A good headline gets things read. It needs to speak to your members and catch their attention. Think solutions. Focus on your reader. Get them reading.

"How to Get Promoted By Working Less" is much more interesting than "May's Meeting."

5. Have a great P.S.

If your headline has done it's job, the second thing your members will look at is your P.S. in a letter. Hit them hard with an irresistible offer here.

6. Every paragraph must inspire action.

Keep your paragraphs short and to the point. You want to keep them reading.

If it's not relevant to your members, delete it.

Your last paragraph should ask for some type of action from your members. Tell them what you want them to do next — sign up, call, fax back, etc.

7. "YOU" is the most important word you can use.

Once you have your first draft done, reread what you have written. Who is it really written to and about? Do you focus on your members' benefits and solutions or on your chapter needs?

Count how many times you used "you" and compare it to how many times you used "I," "we" and "the chapter" in your writing.

If you're short on "you," do some conversions and add more "you" to your writing.

For example, change, "The chapter needs," to "You can <benefit/solution>."

Don't feel bad if there's a lot to change. After many years of practice, I still have to rewrite several sentences every time I put something together.

Increased member involvement is worth the effort.

Get Your Members Involved By Using Testimonials

Using testimonials from peers is powerful strategy for persuading your members it's worth investing their time in your chapter activities.

Using testimonials creates a real win-win.

The members providing the quotes feel important and get their name in print.

The members reading the quotes believe them more than anything you can write — no matter how well you use features, benefits and solutions!

Published testimonials are not ego driven boasting.

They help your members make good decisions about the use of their time.

How do you use testimonials, or quotes, effectively?

Use them anytime you want to persuade your members to take action.

You might use quotes to highlight the value of attending your meetings, working on specific projects, donating to your cause, or getting your certification.

You can use them throughout letters or promotional pieces. You might use them as side bars to articles.

A great quote can even be used as a headline!

• **How do you get people to give you quotes to use?**

If a member writes you a note of thanks, ask them for permission to publish the letter or to use an excerpt in your promotional materials.

The easiest way to get quotes is to ask for them.

1. If someone raves about your chapter, ask them for a quote to use in your next newsletter.

If they say yes, grab a piece of paper and write it down immediately. Remember to spell their name correctly and get their title and company, if appropriate.

2. Collect quotes on your program feedback forms.

Ask an open-ended question like "How will you be able to use this information?"

Have a place on your form where they can check off and give you permission to use their comments for promotional materials.

3. Call specific people and ask for them.

You may want a specific person to endorse what's going on. Call them and ask for a quote. Most people are flattered you asked and eager to help you out.

• **How do you decide which quotes to use?**

It all depends upon what outcomes you want to achieve by using them.

1. Use quotes that reflect the group of people you want to persuade to take action.

You can also target specific groups of members to activate. This group might be new members, old members, women, minorities, senior level, people from out of town or people in town.

It all depends on who you want to have start showing up for events.

2. Use a mix by sex, geography, position and length of membership.

If you have a diverse membership, make sure that diversity is reflected in the quotes you use.

3. Use different people in every newsletter.

More members get their name in print and feel like they are movers and shakers in your chapter — and therefore have to keep showing up.

Secondly, when less active members see different people rave about your events each month, they may show up just to see what everyone is talking about!

4. Use quotes that highlight benefits and solutions.

"I made valuable contacts" or "I impressed my boss with my new skills at work" is much more persuasive than generic comments like, "It was great!" or "The speaker was good."

When people give you generic quotes, ask for more details. Why did they like your meeting? What's the biggest benefit? How has attending helped them?

Get to the meat of what being involved is all about.

That's what people use to decide if participating will give them a good return on their time investment.

- **How long should the testimonies be?**

As a general rule, you should keep quotes as powerful as possible and as short as possible. Think of them as mini-headlines.

However, if you're launching a big campaign, like a foundation drive, you might want to use a full letter.

- **How many should you use?**

Sticking to the rule of three per topic is always a safe bet. It's enough to make an impact.

Several groups of testimonials may be scattered throughout your piece reflecting different things.

You may want to go back and review the comments about using hot buttons in writing. They apply to quotes too.

Good testimonies hit hot buttons and motivate members to continue "buying" the value of being active in your chapter.

Now let's talk about staying in touch with members...

— Chapter Three —

How to Add Value By Staying in Touch

Reach Out with Newsletters

Your chapter newsletter can be one of your greatest assets for showing value of involvement to members — or a complete waste of time and money.

Your newsletter needs to be informative, interesting and fun to read. If not, it competes with junk mail.

5 Tips for Creating Newsletters Your Members Will Love to Read

1. Give appropriate notice for events.

Your members need lead time to be able to plan for attending your events. Work schedules have to be arranged and possibly baby-sitters hired.

It's extremely frustrating to learn about an early bird special registration rate after the cut off date — and, even worse, notice arriving after the event.

To monitor how quickly your newsletters are delivered, always send a copy to yourself. If you mail to a broad area, ask your committee or board members to give you a call when their newsletter arrives.

If one city always arrives late, mail them first class if you are using a bulk rate. It's worth the extra money to respect those members' timelines with due notice.

2. Include a contact person for questions.

Providing a name and phone number for events gives new members a resource to answer their questions — and increases their comfort level to get active.

Include contact information for feature articles as well. Even the best written article may leave questions in your members' minds. Easy access to authors provides a convenience for your members.

3. Let "keepers" help with reporting.

Using "keepers" is an easy way to collect the valuable information people learned at your programs.

Simply put index cards at each table. At the end of the program, ask each person to write down the one or two best ideas ("keepers") that they learned.

Offering a door prize drawn from the turned in cards will help you collect more keepers.

Select the five or ten most common keepers to publish in your newsletter.

It's a nice review for those who attended your program and gives those who didn't attend a taste for the value they missed.

If you get a lot of ideas, mention that these are the top 5 or 10 out of 75 keepers that were turned in. Encourage non-attendees to contact other members to learn more — and to make sure they don't miss the next program!

3. Determine a minimum number of members whose names will be mentioned each month.

Your members love to get their names in print. If you say something nice, they can show their bosses what they've been up to.

Some ways to do this include...

- Thank you's for volunteer work.

- Congratulations on achievements.

- New member interviews.

- Member profiles.

- Birthdays, anniversaries, babies, renewals, etc.

- "I-spy" report on people doing nice things.

- How-to articles by members.

4. Create forums for people to share their ideas in.

Give your members an opportunity to experience a sense of community through your newsletter.

Ideas include:

- Question of the month — and answers.

- A regular page of "the best lessons learned."

- A place to offer and request help.

5. Offer sneak previews for people who help you prepare your newsletters for mailing.

Promoting a sneak preview opportunity implies that there's valuable information to be read each month — creating a positive spin about your paper.

If you fold and stamp your own newsletter for mail, turn the work into a party. It gets more people involved and adds excitement to your publication.

Your Internal Membership Roster

One of the perks of belonging to your chapter is the friendships made among members. Your internal roster is an important tool to fuel this bonding.

- **Keep your roster current.**

Add new member information to your roster and get it in the hands of other members as soon as possible.

Having to wait for the next annual directory to be printed is too long for a new chapter member to have to wait in order to be part of your group.

- **Include networking information.**

You already do this if you are a professional or trade association. Civic and community service groups add extra member value by providing this information.

Encourage your members to remember other members when looking for help.

If you can position your chapter as a strong networking group or the "place for answers," you will see your membership numbers soar.

- **Include areas of strength or mentoring topics.**

A neat way to further encourage relationship building within your chapter is to list an area or two that your members are willing to mentor others in.

You can provide a list of topics for them to chose from related to your membership in order to code listings.

Or, for more variety, and if you have the space, let your members come up with their own areas of expertise.

There's a wealth of information inside of your membership. This listing helps individual members tap into it.

Reach Out with Technology

Technology is a great way to add another point of access for your membership — and save money.

First, you need to figure out how literate your group is when it comes to e-mail and websites. (If few are very advanced, helping members get on-line could be a valuable benefit that your chapter offers.)

While not going to go into any in-depth, how-tos, here are a few things to consider for your chapter.

Your Chapter Website

• **Keep it updated regularly.**

You want your website to be a valuable, time-saving resource for your members.

Consider highlighting new additions to your website in your published newsletter to cross train your members to information sources.

• **Publish your website address regularly.**

Your members need to know where to go. Your address should be listed as often as your chapter phone number or mailing address.

• **Create a members only forum for discussions.**

If you do this, make sure all of your members, including new ones, learn how to access this exclusive privilege for your chapter.

• **Encourage members to submit articles to be published on your website.**

It's another win-win situation. You have less work to do in creating content and you members get some nice exposure in exchange for sharing their expertise.

• **If you don't have a website, consider having one of your members learn how to put it together for you.**

This is a great learning opportunity for one of your members to sharpen their skills — and perhaps help them professionally as well.

You'll need to arrange some board approval over what actually goes on line. But, you would need to do this whether using a member or professional web designer.

Using E-mail with Your Members

• **Carefully compile your members e-mail addresses.**

If someone has e-mail and you leave them off the chapter mailings, it can create a lot of ill will.

• **Use e-mail appropriately.**

It's great for reminders, newsletters, and last minute notices — as long as everyone has it.

If you have members who are not on-line, it's critical to keep them informed and not overlooked.

- **Even technology has bad days.**

Sometimes computers crash or e-mail addresses are accidentally deleted. If you have important information, such as member only opportunities, it needs to go out in hard copy as well as via e-mail.

- **Include phone numbers for "live" people.**

When sending out e-mail notices, make sure there's a contact for a live person. Some people still prefer to use the phone for personal questions.

- **Set up your chapter e-mails so addresses don't show.**

Create a special address or blind carbon copy the addresses so people don't get long messages filled basically with addresses.

One association sent out a simple notice about change of dates. Since it's a large group, it took eight e-mail messages of maximum size filled with addresses in order to include everyone.

This volume clogged members' e-mail boxes.

More bad feelings were created towards the association when a few members used those same lengthy messages for their own e-mail junk mail solicitations.

• **Use e-mail to get quick feedback on member opinions about chapter issues.**

Whether you use the entire membership or a select group, it's a great way to let members contribute to the direction of your chapter — and inspire them to be more active since their voice does count.

Now that you've done your marketing and have your members pumped up with quality communication, let's take a look at face-to-face meetings...

— Chapter Four —

Creating Meetings Your Members Will Love to Attend

Your chapter meetings give your members the chance to meet each other face to face — critical for building that sense of community that so many of them want.

Your members also expect a good return for their time investment — as well as the chance to have some fun and get away from the stress of the day.

Here are some ideas to help you create the meetings your members will love to attend — and keep coming back for more.

First Impressions

1. Make sure you are ready to go when promised.

Your members rearrange their schedules to make it to your events on time. It's important for your greeters and registration people to be ready to greet them.

2. Use easy-to-read name tags.

- **Use name tags at every meeting.**

One chapter made their annual dinner a semi-formal event. To add to the glamour, they decided to also forego name tags that evening.

The room was a buzz with stressed out members who could not remember peoples' names! This frustration really put a damper on a special night.

- **Make first names easy to read from a distance.**

This helps increase members' confidence as they approach each other. It's also much easier for people with bifocals to read.

3. Find a way to identify guests and new members.

Whether you use ribbons, stickers or different colored name tags, help your members to easily identify who is a guest and who is new to your chapter.

- Membership committees can make sure that guests are being introduced to others and not standing alone.

- Less active members are also not mistaken as guests — nor get their feelings hurt for being forgotten.

- Giving special recognition to new members is a nice way to make them extra welcome to your group.

The Social Hour

It's important for you to support your members in building their relationships within your chapter. The more buddies they have, the more likely they are to become long-term, active members.

1. Background music helps ease tension — especially for early arrivals.

Since meeting new people is hard for many, it may take effort just to show up. Music helps dull the intense quiet that adds to peoples' nervousness.

Make sure the volume is loud enough to be heard, but low enough to easily talk over. Think elevator music.

For a special treat, consider booking a local high school music group. Music teachers are thrilled to give their students live exposure — often for a small donation.

Live classical or jazz music creates a wonderful atmosphere for networking at your meeting. Just make sure someone is in charge of keeping their volume at an appropriate level.

2. Have occasional ice-breaker activities.

Help your members mingle by giving them an excuse to talk to each other. There are several ice-breaker activities that you can do.

A fun and easy mixer is "Meeting Bingo." Your members get to find out what they have in common.

Create a regular Bingo grid. Instead of numbers, put some category in each box that is relevant to your members and your chapter.

Some examples include: Current job title, city you work in, favorite book, favorite movie, favorite sport, biggest challenge at work, time in current position, years of membership in chapter, etc.

Players must then find other members who have the same answer as them.

When they find someone with a common answer, they put that person's name in that box. Limit members to using the same person only twice when filling the boxes to encourage more mixing.

Depending upon how much time you have, give prizes for the most Bingos or a full page of matches.

Make your prizes fun to keep in the spirit of the game. One of the best prizes I've given is a magnet that meows — a person who can fill up a sheet in that short of time, really is the cat's meow!

Other ideas include: conversation hearts candy in February, Baby Ruth bar for hitting a home run, cough drops to help recover from all that talking, Cracker Jacks for being an ace networker. Get creative. Your members will love it!

While you don't have to do ice-breakers every meeting, an occasional game or two helps members move beyond their regular friends in your chapter.

3. Use Meeting Hosts.

Meeting Hosts make sure that EVERY member feels welcomed when they arrive.

Their job is more than greeting and shaking hands at the door. It's actually being in the social room and acting as if your meeting is their party.

They can help members get situated, chat with them and introduce them to others.

Acting as a Meeting Host is a also great way for shy people to feel more comfortable meeting others. Their "job" gives them a reason to mingle.

It's nice to have a minimum of one Host for every ten people attending.

Create a Host committee, or open the opportunity up to the general membership. You may find your members scrambling to volunteer. I've seen people sign up 3 - 4 months in advance in order to make sure they get a chance to act as Host!

7 Tips to Better Business Meetings

Long and boring meetings kill chapters.

As important as your chapter business may be, you've got to remember that without WIIFM for your members, there are more important things for them to be doing with their time.

The secret to adding WIIFM is to give your members every chance that you can to participate — and to create excitement about attending your meetings.

1. Introductions are important.

• Your members want to know who's at your meeting. It's worth the time investment to at least let everyone introduce themselves.

• Make sure you send a microphone around during introductions if you meet in a large room or more than 50 people are in attendance.

2. Claims-to-fames are great for smaller chapters.

• When members introduce themselves, ask them to also share their claim-to-fame for the past month — that is, what exciting achievement happened.

• Have the room applaud after each claim-to-fame is announced. This feeling of support can't be beat!

There are few places your members can go and get cheered for taking risks.

• You'll also find that networking after the meeting picks up as your members want to learn the rest of the story for each other's achievements.

3. Launch your meeting by reminding your members what your chapter is all about.

Use your defining statement that you created earlier to help set the mood for the meeting and to get members focused on where they are.

4. Let your pride shine through your meeting.

Enthusiasm is contagious. When you are proud of your chapter and it's accomplishments, your members get excited too!

5. Keep your officer reports short!

- **Give reports a time limit to stick to.**

It will keep the meeting moving along and give your officers a chance to practice effective speaking.

- **Create some hand signal with officers and chairs to tell them when their time is up.**

Make sure people know who the timer is and where they are sitting.

- **Make sure that you don't repeat everything your officers just said as you transition to the next report.**

It's easy to double meeting time with this bad habit!

- **Encourage your officers and teams to get creative with their announcements.**

Skits, rap songs, costumes, music add to your meeting — and keep it more interesting!

- **Clap after every report.**

It makes being an officer or chair more exciting. Also helps keep your members involved in the meeting.

6. If you are not very outgoing, consider having another officer help emcee your meeting.

To run an enthusiastic meeting takes outgoing skills. Your term as chapter leader can be a great opportunity to explore being more outgoing.

If you are uncomfortable with the enthusiasm, that's okay. Just get a more outgoing officer to help emcee your chapter meeting.

You still keep your authority. And, of course, run your board meetings.

You might have your vice president do it or have a different board member each month. This gives them some nice exposure and fuels the meeting pace.

7. Keep your meetings timely.

- **Start on time and end on time.**

Your members planned their time based on your word being good. To start late is disrespectful and running over puts unnecessary pressure on your members.

- **If you see your meeting is running late, warn people in advance.**

This gives them time to make phone calls if needed or to plan at what point they will leave.

You may want to take a short break before the last stretch of your meeting so people who have to leave can do so without feeling bad about walking out.

- **Keep committee discussions at committee meetings.**

There's no need to hash things out at your regular chapter meetings.

- **Put time limits on items that need to be discussed at chapter meetings.**

If things get heated, consider tabling the discussion until the next meeting in order to do some more research on the issue.

- **Work with a timed agenda.**

Using your meeting agenda, decide ahead of time how many minutes each section and report will get. Write expected running clock times in red on the left-hand margin. For example: 7:00 - start meeting; 7:02 - introductions; 7:15 - first report; etc.

Use these times as benchmarks to keep your pace — and adjust as you need to in order to end on time.

Make note of actual times in a different color ink.

Share a copy of your timed agenda for the meeting with your board members before starting.

After the meeting, analyze where you fell off schedule.

What happened? Could this have been avoided or did you just misjudge time?

Is there a particular officer who is too long winded and needs help getting to the point?

It will take a couple of meetings to get your timing down if it's a new skill for you.

Now that you've got the meeting basics down, it's time to move on to programming.

— Chapter Five —

Creating Programs Your Members Will Love to Attend

Professional/personal development is one of the top reasons your members join your chapter.

Great programming can take your chapter to new heights — increased attendance, enthusiastic members who rave about the value of your meetings, and tons of guests who show up with little effort to see what you are all about.

Poor and inconsistent programming creates a negative force — that can impact even the strongest chapters.

The only difference between the highs of great success and the hemorrhaging of membership due to poor programs is strategic planning.

It's your job to help make sure that your chapter provides consistent, quality programming to meet your members needs.

Here's how to do it...

Find Your Defining Programming Statement

In Chapter One, we discussed how to create a defining statement that specifically describes your members.

Now it's time to expand your defining statement to reflect the programs your members need and want — to create your **Defining Programming Statement**.

The easiest way to identify your member needs is to ask them.

Take a quick reading at a meeting. Ask your members, "If you could only do one program this year, what would help them the most?" Have them write down their answers and turn them in.

Review what comes back. Is there a pattern of frequently requested topics? This will help you to start identifying their priorities.

If you get a ton of different topics, compile them into a short check-off survey. Ask members to identify their top three choices.

If you can't do this at a meeting, consider a fax or e-mail survey to speed up requests.

Review your new results. What topics continue to rise to the top as priorities? By now you should be getting a feel for your membership.

Don't stop here! It's time to come up with your defining programming statement.

Try and finish the following statement:

Our programs teach our members how to <result>.

For example, the women business owners group identified that their members were either owners of baby businesses or "pregnant" with an idea and exploring the concept of business ownership.

The most critical thing for any new business is to start making money. This was good, but not a sharp enough focus yet.

The women needed to add an element of urgency.

Their defining programming statement became, "Our programs teach our members how to make more money the next day."

Getting to yes in sales, how to create their own newsletter, how to work with printers, writing killer copy, and networking were all hot topics for them.

Long term financial planning, humor at work, political candidates wanting to talk about their platform, and team building were topics that did not serve this predominantly home-based, growth-orientated group of women.

Once focus is clear, selecting powerful programs for members is easy to do.

It may take you several attempts to get the statement that is right for your group. Keep playing with the words and angles that you approach it from.

Once you get the right statement...

1. Share it with your members.

If it is right, they will get excited about it. Ask them for feedback to make any fine-tuning.

2. Start announcing that this will be the standard for any programs that your group has.

Members get a clear picture of what you are offering in return for their time. They will also be able to help identify potential speakers for programs.

3. If a program does not fit your statement, no matter how interesting it is, do not use it.

By announcing your statement, you have made a promise to your members about what they will get for their time. A program that doesn't fit is like a bait and switch ad — and bad for business!

Hanging tight to your niche will build the reputation of your chapter.

If the inappropriate program is really good, pass the lead on to a more appropriate group in your area.

Negotiate member rates for your members in return for sharing this information with the other group.

5 Tips to Get Some Rhythm for Your Chapter Calendar

Once you have your defining programming statement, you are ready to do some long-range planning — and to give your chapter calendar some rhythm.

1. Plan your programs at least six months out.

You need this much time to plan for the variety in your programs that creates the rhythm.

Extra bonus — your members appreciate the advance notice so they can plan better to attend your meetings.

2. Vary the types of topics you cover month to month.

For example, vary your calendar by the type of skill covered. A "hard" skill topic like technology might follow a "soft" skill like how to build relationships.

The key is to make your members feel like they are attending a new program every month — not the same thing over and over.

3. Vary the style of presentation.

Don't have just a string of lectures. There are many options out there that will make your meetings more interesting! We'll cover various formats in a minute.

4. Vary the level of the topic presented.

Have some programs approach the big picture and others go deep. Consider adding advanced skills or futuristic topics to your mix.

This variety helps your members stretch their minds.

5. Always consider what else is taking place at your meetings each month.

When planning your programming calendar, write down all of the "must do's" before assigning programs to a particular month.

Your members have limited time. In heavy business months, plan for shorter programs.

If all of your months look heavy, it's time for some reevaluation about what's really necessary and how to lighten your load.

6 Different Formats for Your Programs

There are many ways to format programs for your chapter and you want to vary them month to month. This list covers the traditional to the cutting edge which makes your members active participants.

1. Basic lecture — also known as "Talking Heads"

This is the traditional speaking format. Your members are passive learners. Unless the speaker is very dynamic and tells interesting stories, this format can put your members to sleep.

2. An Interactive Speaker

This person gets your members involved in learning of the topic covered. You'll see members talking in groups, role playing and doing activities that the speaker facilitates.

Your members get to build relationships as they learn important information — and, you're hitting two important hot buttons!

Ask potential speakers how they will get your members involved in their talks. If they don't know, look for another speaker.

3. Round Tables of Answers

Members love these programs. Each table features a certain topic and members get to share their wisdom with each other.

Sample topics include: industry issues, best lesson learned this year, biggest challenge to overcome, etc.

For an hour program, have your members shift tables three times. A facilitator should explain time limits and help with transitions.

A nice touch is to have the facilitator close the meeting by having members share some of the "ah-has" they learned during the hour.

4. Meet the Pros Program

Same concept as round tables — except, instead of members sharing ideas in a free-for-all, an "expert" shares their wisdom with the small group for their time together.

Promote the topics in advance to give your members time to think about what they want to learn.

To run the program: Have numbers on each table correlating with an expert. Members get to talk to three experts in an hour.

Make sign up sheets for each rotation in different colors. Example: Round #1 - Yellow; #2 - Green; # 3 - Orange.

Each sign up sheet should have eight pull tabs per session to limit size of the group. List the speaker and table number on the tab.

Ask your members to take a pull tag for one expert for each session. They should have three different colored slips in their hands when done.

Use a facilitator to explain rules, ease table changes and summarize the experience.

5. 60 Answers in 60 Minutes

This is a fast and fun program to run at your chapter meeting. Everyone gets involved — and gets some great take-aways too.

Each member gets 60 seconds to share their best idea about a topic that reflects your defining programming statement guidelines.

Examples include: Best ideas for building teams, best ideas for managing stress, best ideas for increasing sales, best ideas from the Internet, etc.

Make sure you promote your topic ahead of time to give members the opportunity to think of good ideas to share with each other.

If you only have 20 members, everyone can share their three best ideas.

Since these ideas will be fast and furious, you may want to find a way to record the program.

Another approach: Have everyone write down their idea on a 3" X 5" card to be compiled for later distribution to attendees.

Point to consider: If you don't provide the full set of tips, members will have to attend in order to get the benefit of all these great ideas.

Either way, make sure you leave time for networking after your meeting so members can get details from each other.

6. A "Solutions for You" Program

There will be a lot of one-on-one interaction for your members with this program.

Each member writes down a question they would like to explore possible solutions for.

They might search for answers to a problem, suggestions for their next career step, or sources for a new supplier.

A facilitator starts the program by having the room get in groups of three with people they don't know well.

Give them about eight minutes to share with each other their questions and possible solutions.

Have members switch into new groups at the end of each time limit. Allowing for transition time, your groups should shift about every 10 minutes.

This program is another double hitter. Your members will get a list of possible solutions for their questions — and some new buddies in your chapter as well.

How to Find Speakers For Your Programs

1. Create a speaker proposal form.

Print your defining programming statement at the top.

Ask potential speakers questions such as: What topic would your like to speak on? What key points will be covered? How does your program apply to our defining statement? How will you get our members involved in your program?

Give every board member a copy of this form to distribute to people who approach them about presenting to your chapter.

Review completed forms with your calendar rhythm in mind. If a topic fits your defining statement, where does that type of program fit in your calendar?

2. Possible sources for speakers

• Your members — They have a wealth of wisdom to share. Just make sure they fit what you need. They are also a great referral source.

• The local Chamber of Commerce — Many of them have a list of speakers or a speakers bureau.

• Local colleges often have bureaus.

• Many non-profits also have bureaus.

• Your local chapter of the National Speakers Association. www.nsa.org

3. Professional speakers versus public speakers

Public speakers are usually free or charge a low honorarium. They speak as a hobby or as part of their paid job. The quality of programs varies widely.

Professional speakers make their living by speaking. Their fees are generally thousands of dollars plus expenses. (Beginning speakers may charge in the hundreds of dollars.)

You are paying professional speakers for their expertise in both what they say and how they say it.

If you work with a professional speaker, you want to find one who will tailor their speech to your group. They should want to learn more about your members and the challenges they face.

The best way to guarantee the quality of a speaker is to see them in person. If you can't see them, a demo tape will give you a feel for their energy level, their style and how they work with the audience.

If you want a particular professional speaker, but can't afford their fee:

• **Try and find some sponsors for the speaker.**

You can give your sponsors special exposure to your members. Let them do a short info-mercial about themselves before they introduce your speaker. Give your sponsor a special information table at the event.

• **Find another chapter to share the cost with you.**

Perhaps it's time to have that joint meeting you've been talking about. Consider other chapters of your association or working with other local chapters.

• **Get other bookings in the area for the speaker.**

You will be able to share travel costs. Your speaker may be willing to "credit" your cost with some "commission" for the extra bookings.

- **Explore the option of trade with your speaker.**

What can you offer them that's equal to the value of their program? Can you include their spouse on an extended vacation in your area? Do you have members able to donate services or gift certificates?

You'll need to get creative. Look at a package that's equivalent to the program cost — and is of value to your potential speaker.

- **Ask them to refer a speaker who is in your budget and covers a similar topic.**

Many professionals know other speakers in different price ranges that they can recommend to you.

Good programming takes time — and your members enthusiasm about your meetings is worth the effort.

Now, let's take a look at how your leadership style can help reach Generation Me...

Chapter Six

Leading the Way for Generation Me

Generation Me is a take-action type of group.

They look for return on their investment of time — and, with the right leadership, are willing to step up for even more involvement. Without it, they will leave your chapter for a better use of time.

There's a lot riding on you and your actions this year.

As a leader of your chapter, YOU are the association to your members.

You see the big picture of what is going on. It's your job to share this with your members and sell them on the importance of being active in your chapter.

Recruitment. Active members. Retention. Enthusiasm about being involved. **It's the R.A.R.E. way.**

When you focus on creating active members and building enthusiasm about your chapter, recruitment and retention happen naturally.

The 13 Keys to the R.A.R.E. Leader Way

1. Decide your legacy at the beginning of your term.

You're making a big commitment to your chapter. If you're like most leaders, it's going to be a year-long ride on a roller coaster — packed with highs and lows, sudden drops and the thrill of a lifetime!

Plan today how you want to be remembered.

What will your year stand for? When your members talk about your year in office, how will they describe it?

Did you help the chapter become financially strong? Was it during your year that the chapter grew like crazy? Did you open the door to a better reputation in your community at large?

Successfully creating a legacy makes all of the energy that you put in your chapter this year a worthwhile investment for your time.

You'll get that subtle, confident glow of someone who knows how to do great things.

So, what will your legacy be? How will you leave your mark on your chapter?

2. Start training your potential replacements as soon as you take office.

One of your jobs as a chapter leader is to mentor your potential replacements throughout your term.

The more you help them learn about leadership with you at their side, the easier it will be for them to step up to the plate to fill your shoes.

Doing this will also give you more people to delegate more work to during your term.

Don't just work with next year's leaders. Start thinking years in advance. Develop the leadership of members new and old.

Leadership is an important skill to use with your chapter and at work. By sharing your experience, you make your members' time more valuable when spent with you.

3. Check your troubles at the door.

It doesn't matter what went on before you walk into a chapter event.

The minute you hit that door, you need to be "on" — representing your association and chapter to all.

Some days this will be tougher than others. Find ways that work for you to quickly blow off steam so you can ease into your leader mode.

Happy music in your car, a quick round of jumping jacks, quiet meditation, or a cup of tea. It doesn't matter how you do it — as long as it works.

4. Be a role model for your members and board.

What you do speaks louder than what you say.

If you ask your board to mingle more with members, be out there working the room. Make the right decisions and share why you do it with others.

You never know who's watching you — and who will go into a totally unrelated situation using your words and actions.

It's a gift you give your chapter.

5. Fuel your members' aspirations.

As a chapter leader, you also become a head cheerleader for your members. Help your members to step up to leadership opportunities and get involved in your chapter and their career.

Be proud of your members' accomplishments. Cheer them on their path.

Your members are looking for a community to belong to. With someone like you as a leader, they're bound to stick around!

6. Attach your enthusiasm to your chapter.

Your members need to link your enthusiasm about what's going on in your chapter to your chapter — rather than attach it to you.

It's a matter of survival for your chapter.

You want as many members as possible enthusiastic about your chapter. If they see this enthusiasm only as part of your term of office, they may drift off after you step down. After all, the excitement will be gone.

By teaching members to see the wonderful things in your chapter, they will continue to find enthusiasm whether you are there or not.

You want to constantly build for the long life and success of your chapter.

Doing so, makes you a R.A.R.E. Leader indeed.

7. Keep a balance in your chapter between cliques and being inclusive for all.

Your members, especially the older ones, will have their circles of close friends — or cliques.

These relationships are important and help to keep them coming back to your meetings year after year.

On the other hand, new members also need to be welcomed into your chapter by all of your members.

As you oversee your chapter calendar for the year, plan opportunities for old friends to hang out and new friendships to be started.

Including new members may be as simple as asking an older member to help you out.

Older members may not step up because they figure you have it covered — or have forgotten what being a new member feels like.

When you personally ask them to help you out by hosting a newer member at a meeting, they are often glad to help — and feel needed again.

8. Be a great communicator.

Communicate with your board and members what's going on with your chapter as much as you can. Don't be a lone ranger.

Being in touch makes your members feel like they are part of a community — one of the big hot buttons for being an active member of your chapter.

For example, a chapter annually holds a presidential holiday party in December. It's a nice gathering and spouses get a chance to meet all the players.

One year, the party was canceled with no notice to general members.

Shouldn't be a big deal, since it was never announced as happening and appeared on no calendars, right?

WRONG! Throughout December members quietly wondered why they had been left out of the big annual event. Some even felt rejected by the chapter.

As members talked about the "missing party," the spin grew on what a bad year it was for the association.

What should have happened?

Good communication would have nipped this problem in the bud.

People may have been disappointed, but they wouldn't be talking about the death of the chapter.

The board members should have told members the party was canceled that year. A reason would have been nice as well.

Instead, this board had an uphill climb to rebuild the trust and relationship with its members.

9. Identify the influencers in your chapter.

Your chapter has a group of people who influence blocks of members. They may not be "official" leadership of your chapter, but they can definitely rally the troops.

Turn these people into your champions.

Help them to stay active. If they're not officers, use them as occasional sounding boards and thank them for their time.

If they feel appreciated and respected by you, they will help make sure you have a successful year.

This is also true for people who ran for office and lost. Help them to save face and stay active in your chapter. They may be your great leaders of future boards.

10. Make your word golden.

If you say you will do something, do it.

If you can't live up to it, let people know so they can plan around it.

Don't leave your members hanging on a short rope.

Avoid stretching the truth with your members. Secrets get exposed and lies will catch up with you. Once trust is broken, it's hard to get back.

Remember, you represent your chapter and association to your members.

11. Stand behind your board and chairs publicly.

There's nothing worse than a leader who complains vocally about board members and chairs to other members. This includes past boards too.

It creates bad blood and makes you look like a cad.

If you have a problem, talk to that person in private.

If you need help working things out, turn to past presidents or your association leadership for help.

If you need a sounding board to blow steam find a confidant and do it in private.

The best confidants do not belong to your chapter and can give you unbiased feedback about what they hear.

12. Learn to work with people different than you.

It takes many sets of skills to run a successful chapter —
and no one type of person has them all.

Beef up your skills of talking to members with different
backgrounds and skills than you. Perhaps this skill
building could even be a chapter program.

Ask people to explain what you don't understand. Ask
why things work. Respect your members differences.

A well-rounded team can accomplish great things.

13. Make time for your personal life in the midst of your leadership experience.

There's a temptation with leadership to make your
chapter a higher priority than anything else.

**Don't do it. If you are not a "full" person, you have
less to give back to your chapter.**

Be a good delegator and give others a chance to lead
temporarily. Train them for future success.

Make dates with your spouse. Take time to pay your
bills and attend your daughter's graduation.

**Your members need a leader and role model who has
the delicate balance they need in their lives too.**

Now let's get mixing with your members...

— Chapter Seven —

Strategic Mixing With Your Members

As a chapter leader, networking takes on a whole new meaning. It's no longer carefree visiting.

When members talk with you, they feel connected to the whole chapter — and like they belong.

A few minutes of caring conversation with you can make their day.

It may sound funny, but as a chapter leader you've become a VIP of sorts — and your members love to be friends with important people like you.

There's another benefit as well...

Mingling with your members is also an opportunity for you to ask some quick questions and learn how well you're hitting their hot buttons.

When it's social hour, you need to be on a mission of strategic interactions reaching out to your members — and hearing what they have to say.

Getting Ready to Go

1. Polish your networking skills.

You need to feel comfortable making small talk and working a room.

If this does not come naturally for you, don't worry. It's just a set of skills that anyone can learn. Hopefully your association will provide you with some training.

If you need a quick refresher, check out my book, *Networking: The Skill the Schools Forgot to Teach.* (Available at www.peoplepowerunlimited.com.)

2. Set some goals before each event.

Decide in advance how many people you will meet and what you hope to learn from networking.

Try to talk to at least one person for every five minutes of networking time.

For example, your goal would be to talk to six people during 30 minutes of networking.

Plan to take the pulse of your membership. Create questions to ask your members about key issues you're facing with your chapter.

The key is to plan in advance and ask questions that can be easily answered — this is, after all, a social hour.

Setting goals will help you maximize your time.

3. Read the attendance sheet before your members start arriving.

Looking over the names will help you to remember them when you see your members in person.

This review also gives you a chance to pick out a few people you want to be sure to talk to — such as new members or people who have not attended your meetings lately.

7 Tips for More Effective Mixing with Members

1. Be prepared to work the room.

When your meeting's networking time starts, you need to be ready to mix with your members.

Arrive a few minutes early if you need time to get yourself orientated.

It's a drag when the chapter leadership comes in unprepared for a meeting and is too busy to talk to anyone there.

It's also easier for the membership committee to turn a guest into a new member when leaders take time to welcome them to the chapter meeting.

2. Pretend you're hosting a party.

If you get nervous networking, pretend you're hosting a party instead. Your focus is on making your guests (members) feel welcomed and comfortable.

By shifting your attention to your members' comfort and off how well you are doing, you'll be more relaxed.

3. Help your members make connections.

As a chapter leader, you know what's going on with many of your members. Get good at introducing them to each other.

Help your members hook up with others who have common interests or with members who can help them solve a problem.

Think of yourself as a referral source to your members.

The more connections members make at meetings, the more value they get from being active in your chapter.

4. Train your members to introduce people to you.

Let your members know you want to meet their friends and guests. Your caring makes them feel important for bringing new people to meetings.

When you are excited about meeting new people, it makes your chapter feel more inclusive — and like a warm community.

5. Do not hang out with other officers.

When you do, you create the feeling that your board is a bunch of elitists — not the right image for a chapter who wants members to feel like they belong.

Social hour at your meetings is a time to mix and mingle with general members. You'll see your board buddies later.

6. If you are short with someone, make sure you apologize to them immediately.

Everyone has an occasional bad day in spite of best efforts — it's part of being human.

If you find yourself short with a member due to your bad day, apologize immediately.

If you don't realize how short you were until you get home, give your member a call as soon as it is appropriate to do so and apologize.

"I'm sorry I was short with you. I had a rough day and let it loose on you. I apologize, you deserve better from me," will mend walls and show people you are a caring human — and a wonderful role model.

Not apologizing can spread bad blood through your chapter very quickly. Rude leaders are not popular. Plus, as you may know, people will tell ten people about a bad experience and one about a good one.

A bad day, without an apology, can do a lot of damage.

7. Clip business card corners to remember promises.

When you promise to do something for a member, you need to make sure you do it.

An easy way to remember to call someone is to ask for one of their cards — even if you know them well.

Write on the back of it what you promise to do if you need more of a memory prompt for later.

Casually bend the corner of the card as you put it in your pocket containing the other business cards you have picked up that day.

At the end of your meeting, pull the cards out of your pocket and make note to take quick action on the cards with the clipped corners.

Now that you've been mixing with members it's time show them that you care with a Personal Touch...

— Chapter Eight —

The Secrets of Personal Touch Leadership

When your members get active in your chapter, they give up doing something else.

Help your members feel like they made the right decision — and are valued — by showing that you care with Personal Touch Leadership.

Leaders who focus on Personal Touch have active members who are proud to be part of their chapter.

Here are some ideas to help you reach out with a Personal Touch for your members.

Reach Out By Mail

1. You need to have postcards for your chapter.

Postcards are a quick and easy way to stay in touch. They also cost less to mail.

Create some special postcards to use with your chapter.

Use an 8 1/2" X 11" piece of paper to create a master with four postcards on it. Run them off at a nearby copy center on colorful card stock.

On the "picture" side: Put something meaningful that might go on someone's bulletin board. It could be your theme for the year, quotes that you are famous for, or something that reflects your chapter and association.

Make them fun to receive.

On the other side, run a line down the center to divide the message half from the address half. (Make sure it's big enough to hold a mailing label just in case.)

For example, the message half of my personal postcard has my company name and slogan at the top and my return address, including email and website address, on the bottom.

Leaving just enough room for a couple of sentences makes this type of contact easy to do.

My "picture" side has a variety of R.A.R.E. Leadership Tips on it. I used four different tips on my master to be able to select special messages for different people.

When you run your postcards off at the printer, make sure you ask them to cut your copies into fourths to get a clean edge to your postcards.

Making your cards makes messages more personal.

2. Different ways to use your postcards.

• Thank you notes

It just takes a moment to thank a member. Your appreciation of their efforts makes them more likely to help out again.

• Welcome — Nice to meet you notes

Dropping a line to guests is a powerful statement about what type of chapter you run — friendly.

Since finding a community is a hot button for some, this is an easy way to show potential members they've come to a group that wants them to belong.

• Congratulation notes

When you hear about member achievements, drop them a note.

When I was named an Outstanding Young Michigander, many of the associations that I belong to ran blurbs in their newsletters.

Only one group sent a personal note. It said, "Congratulations on your award. I am so proud that you are a member of our association." It was signed by the President.

You can make your members feel very special with little notes like these. And, when members feel special, they become your champions.

- **Good to see you note**

A quick note to a member who shows up after a long absence is a nice reinforcement about how important they are to your chapter.

- **"Missed you" note**

If you haven't seen someone in awhile, a "missed you" note is a neat touch.

Make your message caring rather than guilt inspiring.

"I've missed your laugh at our meetings. Hope all is well," is much better than, "This is the fourth meeting you've missed. I hope you plan to come back to the group. We need your help."

3. Create a system to make it easy to do.

- Keep a supply of postcard stamps on hand.

- Keep a copy of your roster with your stamps.

- Write 2-3 post cards every day at a regular time.

Being in the habit of sending your postcards out on a regular basis makes it seem like less work. You will also train your mind to see contact opportunities.

The five minute investment that you make writing these cards will help guarantee an easier year as chapter leader for you.

Show You Care at Your Meetings

As a chapter leader, you have the ability to single out some of your members and thank them publicly for their help.

Many people yearn for recognition in their life. Take advantage of your ability to showcase your members.

Give them a token along with the praise.

This gives them proof to show others as well as a solid reminder that you think they are important.

Some easy ideas include:

- **A certificate**

You can buy certificate paper in volume and print them on your computer.

- **Lifesavers — the candy**

Symbolic gifts can be powerful!

When I was president of a chapter, one of the most exciting parts of my meeting was giving out the monthly Lifesaver award.

I would choose a flavor that somehow reflected the special help the honor member provided and tell quite the tale of how they stepped up to help me.

For example: Lemon flavor for helping me get out of a "lemon" of a situation. Tropical flavor for giving me a much needed vacation.

Orange flavor was for "Orange" you glad that Joe helped and you didn't have to — great for very sticky situations and hard work.

My members never knew what angle I would take and it was always a mystery as to who was the winner.

This became so popular, we turned it into a contest.

I would announce the flavor of the month at the beginning of the meeting. Members would write down what they thought the flavor stood for and who should get the award.

I would read the handful of guesses to the chapter — now recognizing even more people. And then, give my version of the award.

If anyone figured out my angle and honoree, they also got Lifesavers.

This was a fun way to end our meetings — and made a lot of people feel good.

• Flowers

A single rose or even carnation adds a special touch to your presentation.

Anything can work when you give it meaning.

5 Tips for Getting Your Board Involved

Your board members can also be key people in reaching out to your members.

1. Create monthly "Hot" lists.

As a board, create a monthly "Hot" list of members you haven't seen in awhile.

Make the total number listed equal to one or two times the number of people who sit on your board.

Assign one or two people for each board member to call. Their goal is to say hello, find out what's going on with your member, and invite them to an upcoming chapter event.

When members have missed many chapter events, it can feel both intimidating and awkward to return to your chapter.

As the discomfort grows and the personal connection to your chapter weakens, other time options become a bigger priority for your members.

These phone calls help to reconnect your members making their return easier to do and a higher priority.

2. Create a phone tree to call members about meetings.

You may wonder why your board needs to take time to call adults to remind them about your meetings — especially when you send them newsletters and the meeting day never changes!

There's truth to all of that.

There's also the bigger truth that your members have a ton of options for their time — and the personal contact can't be beat!

Test it for yourself...

Look at your current level of attendance without calls.

For the next three months, make sure every member gets a personal call reminding them about the meeting and updating them on what's going on.

Add general members as callers if you need to lighten people's loads and keep the time required reasonable.

The members involved will feel more committed to your chapter as well.

Make sure you have someone check results.

If a person can't make their calls for some last minute reason, encourage them to call a back-up person.

Compare the difference in results.

My bet is that you'll see a steady increase in the level of members active in your chapter over the 90-day test.

3. Write handwritten notes on the outside of your chapter newsletters.

Any type of personal contact reaches people and gives them a reason to be active in your chapter.

There was an attendance problem with one of the chapters I served as president.

One day, I helped out my newsletter editor and put together the monthly mailing.

As I read over the names on the labels, I got very frustrated. I liked a lot of those people and didn't understand why they weren't showing up any more.

I decided to do take some action.

On the outside of each newsletter, I wrote:

> *Hi <name>!*
> *Hope to see you at the meeting next week!*
> *Cynthia*

I didn't know if it would make any difference, but at least I felt better.

Little did I know then the power of short messages!

Next week, at the meeting, my jaw hit the ground as member after member walked through the door.

Our attendance was up 50% that night!

My board was amazed and revitalized!

We worked hard to get those "long-gone" members who showed up for that meeting involved once more with our chapter — and succeeded with most.

I've used little notes like that several times since — each time with similarly spectacular results.

Now let's talk about a very special group of people in your chapter — new members!

— Chapter Nine —

How to Turn New Members Into Long-Term Members

Your new members made a decision to turn down other options based on the great return you promised to give them for the investment of their time.

The clock is ticking...

It's time to make your word good.

Your new members are looking for proof that they made a good decision.

This need for reassurance to avoid "buyer's remorse" happens any time a sale is made.

You need to make new members feel welcome and help them get involved in your chapter — and do it as soon as possible.

WARNING: After 90 days with no involvement by a new member, odds are good you'll never see them and they will not renew.

6 Ways to Make New Members Feel Welcome

1. Send them a welcome letter.

Whether a formal letter, handwritten note on your chapter postcards, or a quick e-mail, the form you use doesn't matter. It's the thought that counts.

- **Make it easy to do.**

Keep a form letter on your computer that only needs name and address inserted.

- **Send it as soon as they join.**

A speedy welcome makes your chapter seem excited to include new members.

This quick action also makes them feel like an important addition to the chapter.

- **Set up a system to get contact information.**

Work with the person who gets the checks and applications. Create a systematic way to get new names to you as soon as possible.

Remember to send this information just as quickly to others who are part of the new member welcoming team as well.

2. Introduce new members in your newsletter.

• Include contact information.

You want to make sure your current members can start networking with new members as soon as possible.

• Include some personal information.

A paragraph or two can be interesting to read and helps your current members get a better feel for which new members they want to seek out.

You might include: hobbies, adventures, why they joined, or what they do.

• Mention the person who recruited them.

It's a simple way to give some recognition to members who are helping out.

May also inspire others who want to see their name in print to start recruiting.

• Do it in a timely manner.

If you run a monthly announcement, get new members in it as soon as possible.

Being left out of a new member listing can make a person feel rejected by your chapter.

If it's going to take a month or more delay, communicate this with the new members affected.

3. Hold a new member orientation.

If your chapter uses a lot of alphabet soup names or has a lot traditional activities, a new member orientation can help people feel more confident and included.

• Keep orientations short and interesting.

Attending this orientation should not be a painfully long lecture on how great the group history is and details about everything you do.

The goal is to help your members understand the basics of what's going on and how to get involved.

• Include time to answer their questions.

Your chapter has many "rules" that you may no longer even think about as being an issue.

Dress codes for events, when to bring spouses and significant others, how to host a guest at a meeting are just a few questions your new members may have.

• Hold orientations regularly.

If you have new members monthly, hold orientations monthly to help your members out.

A simple way to do it: Ask new members to arrive 15 - 30 minutes early for a meeting.

Have one of your board members go over important information and answer their questions.

4. Have your members make a debut at the first meeting they attend as a new member.

Give your new members a minute or two to introduce themselves to your chapter.

• Make sure you give advance warning.

Your new members will want to make a good first impression. Planning time will also help them to ease their nerves.

• Applaud when they are done.

Public speaking can be tough for people. The applause helps to welcome them and reward them for taking their first risk with your chapter.

5. Drive new members to their first meeting.

Help new members ease into attending meetings by having members offer to pick them up — whether a five-minute or two-hour drive to the meeting.

It's intimidating to walk into meetings alone when you know few people.

Getting a chance to chat with their driver will add to their confidence.

This strategy may not be appropriate for all chapters, but it's a powerful way to activate new members.

6. Large chapters — hold a new member reception.

This is a special reception to welcome new members into your chapter and to give them a chance for some one-on-one with board members and association VIPs.

• Have them once a quarter.

Once or twice a year is not enough. You need to catch people while they still feel new.

Monthly receptions are an unnecessary drain on your board members. Orientations held during the other eight months will take care of immediate needs.

• Make it a special event.

Send out a special invitation even if the reception takes place on the same day your regular meeting.

Ask for an RSVP and call the new members you do not hear from. Make them all feel included.

• Make new members the VIPs for the event.

Encourage your board to meet as many new members in attendance as possible.

Your board should approach the new members to ease their nerves — rather than wait to be approached.

This is also a great time for board members to recruit new members to work on their committees.

5 Ways to Help Activate Your New Members

It takes time to build trust and comfort in any relationship — including the relationships your new members are creating with your chapter.

Here are some ideas to help the process along and activate your new members.

1. Create a new member welcome kit.

- **It should include:**

A current directory, another welcome letter, details about membership benefits — including passwords to the member only section of your website, a current newsletter, and how to get involved.

- **You may also want to include:**

Some association and chapter history, a glossary if you use a lot of alphabet soup terms, an article about how to build their network by getting involved.

- **Include new member profile sheets.**

Request basic information as well as some information about their interests.

Have new members fax it back to you or include a stamped envelope to make returning it easy to do.

- **Get it out fast!**

The sooner your members get this information, the sooner they feel comfortable getting involved.

2. Have a "guidance counselor" call them.

Get enthusiastic members to call and personally welcome new members to your chapter.

- **Have the "counselors" explore why the new member joined and what might be a good committee for them to get involved with.**

Provide the new member with names and numbers of appropriate committee chairs.

- **Forward interested new member contacts to chairs.**

New members may be shy about calling chairs to volunteer. This way your chairs can take the first step and tap into new member interest sooner.

3. Approach new members in many different ways over a period of time.

Too often there's a big effort for a new member's first month of membership — after that, they are left to navigate on their own.

- **Being a new member can be overwhelming.**

Remembering names, doing the right thing, and getting involved all at once is hard.

No one can remember everything their first month.

• Create a first year program with regular contact to these members.

The American Society of Association Executives (ASAE) sent me a wonderful fax about three months into my membership. It was filled with contact names and numbers and reviewed opportunities for my new involvement in ASAE.

• Survey your first year members at six months to see how you are doing.

Ask what's the most valuable thing they've gotten out of involvement in your chapter and what else they would like to see done.

• Try a quarterly special mailing to first year members that explains some details about what's happening in the months ahead.

For example: dress codes for different events, how the election process works, why your chapter chose a particular fund-raiser, etc.

4. Teach new members how to network.

One of the big hot buttons for joining is to be part of a community — and this means networking.

• The challenge is, in spite of being a top priority, many of your members never learned how to network — meeting new people can be torture for them.

To keep them as members, you need to help them become successful networkers.

• **Include networking tips in new member kits and in your newsletter.**

There is a whole series of articles on networking that you may use for your newsletters posted at my website, www.peoplepowerunlimited.com.

• **Provide networking training for members.**

There are many skills involved in networking — such as mingling with confidence, starting conversations with anyone, building rapport, and giving unforgettable introductions just to name a few.

Weave some form of networking skill training into your programming each year.

These programs should be very interactive. Members love the "safe" opportunity to talk to people they don't know well.

5. Get your board involved.

• **Provide them with a monthly list of new members.**

Make sure you include contact information on this list. You may want to also provide your board with copies of new member profiles.

Board members should keep these lists in a folder to be able to return them in the future as well.

- **Review the list of new members and discuss how to tap into their skills.**

Your new members bring a wealth of talent to your chapter. Make sure to tap into it whenever possible to strengthen your chapter as you activate your members.

- **Review lists again at three months out.**

Assign board members to personally call new members who have yet to show up for anything.

It's hard for a new member to show up out of the blue after 90 days of nothing.

This friendly introduction call will attempt to reconnect the member to your chapter and motivate them to attend a meeting.

You'll look at two lists each month — the current new members and the three month list.

Doing this will add some time to your board meeting, but the increased numbers of active members will make lighter work for everyone — and be worth every minute spent!

Now let's take a look at the skills it takes to manage all of your eager volunteers...

— Chapter Ten —

How to Delegate With Confidence — and Ease

Creating successful, happy volunteers is the key to building an active membership for your chapter.

Delegating with confidence and ease is the skill that makes it all happen.

On the flip side, a poor delegator is a deadly poison to your group.

It's your job as a chapter leader to role model good delegation and to teach all of your chairs this critical skill for smooth volunteer management as well.

15 Tips for Easier Delegation

1. The best way to get power is to share it with many.

Power is not something to hold close to your chest. Share it with others. The more you delegate, the more you can achieve. Power and prestige will follow.

2. Break deadlines down into smaller steps.

As the delegator, you manage the calendar and deadlines. Your chief job is to keep the pace of the project moving ahead — not do all the work yourself!

Delegating can be scary. If someone drops the ball, it can mess everything up and you may have to scramble in a crisis driven response.

• To avoid that scenario, break big deadlines into smaller steps and periodically check in to see how people are doing.

Smaller steps make it easier for busy people to volunteer. It's also easier to nip problems in the bud.

• As you make these mini-deadlines, add a cushion of extra time in at the end in case someone gets slowed down or you need to step in to help.

3. Become an ace at follow up.

• Have a master file where you document the commitments of your volunteers.

Write down who offered to do what and when their work will be done.

At the end of your committee meeting, do a quick review to make sure everyone agrees with what's going to happen.

Send everyone a copy so they can see it in writing.

• **Ask your volunteers to check in as mini-deadlines come up or their work is done.**

If you don't hear from them 24 hours after a deadline, give them a call to see how they are doing.

Assume they are doing their work and just got delayed in talking to you. Never accuse volunteers of not doing their responsibility when you make these calls .

The time they give you is a gift — not a requirement.

• **Encourage your members to contact you if life throws them a curve ball and they will not be able to meet their commitment to the project.**

You or someone else can pick up their work.

When volunteers do call with the bad news, thank them profusely for giving you notice and offer to help them if it is appropriate.

Your members will remember how you treated them the next time you ask for help.

4. Respect people's schedules.

Give people enough notice to get things done in a timely manner that can fit in their schedule.

Emergency rushes should only happen in dire circumstances — not be a standard way of doing business on your committee!

5. Work smart — don't reinvent the wheel.

It's easier to edit something than start from scratch.

Try to find some history if your project has been run before. Talk to past chairs and ask what potential challenges you should look out for.

• If this is a new experience for your chapter, do you have any **members** with relevant professional experience to use as advisors?

• Do you know someone from **another chapter** that's worked on this type of project?

• Do you know someone **in the community**, perhaps in a different organization, who you could talk to?

• Is there a **how-to book** on the subject that you could use as a reference?

The goal in these questions is to get an educated starting point from which to create your committee's own interpretation of the event.

The advice helps you to move faster and avoid things that might trip up your committee — such as needing special permits from your city, state sales tax forms, etc.

6. Encourage a balanced approach rather than martyrdom from your volunteers.

This project may be the center focus of your chapter involvement. Your members are simply helping out.

- **Be aware of the other commitments and events going on in your chapter.**

Don't plan a big committee meeting the day before or after your chapter meeting.

Don't allow your committee work to cannibalize other major chapter activities.

- **The week of a big event can be hectic. Planning the event should be well paced.**

Your committee members should not feel like they are missing out on life over long periods of time due to working on your project.

7. Maximize your volunteers' time contribution.

If you have a work meeting, make sure you do as much as possible while people are there.

- **Plan carefully to have everything ready to go when your volunteers arrive.**

Not being ready is disrespectful and a waste of their time. They may not show for your next meeting.

- **Make sure you have enough work to keep everyone busy who shows up.**

Guestimate how long it would take one person to do the work. Divide it by the number of hours you expect your work meeting to last. That is the number of volunteers you need to show up.

For example: If you need to address 200 envelopes and it takes about 2 minutes per envelope, the total time to complete this work would be about 400 minutes.

400 minutes = about 7 hours with one person working. (400 minutes divided by 60 minutes in an hour)

If you want to have a quick one hour work meeting, you would need 7 volunteers to address 200 envelopes in an hour.

Don't let 10 people sign up to help unless you are going to have additional work for them to do.

People rearrange their schedules to work in your meetings. Make sure everyone has something to do.

• **If you have a lot of little stuff to do, create a joint committee work meeting.**

For example, stuff envelopes at the same time for a couple of different projects. It's a fun way to mix across committees and get a lot done.

You'll need to coordinate your volunteer sign up and work to be done with other chairs.

8. Involve many; drain none.

Break your committee work down into small chunks that can fit into anyone's schedule.

Think in terms of an 30 - 90 minutes top per chunk.

Food for thought: If you ask a member for more than they are really comfortable with, they may be reluctant to turn you down because they don't want to disappoint you.

Don't put them in this position.

If a member takes on a bigger commitment, encourage them to delegate some of the work to other members of the committee and your chapter at-large.

Draining members with huge all consuming pieces of your project makes others reluctant to volunteer for committee work.

9. Keep your committee meetings short.

Create an agenda for your meeting and stick to it. Start on time and end on time.

Use technology to keep in touch and get questions answered. E-mail discussions take place at the convenience of your member.

When you meet with your committee face-to-face, make every minute count.

10. Just because it's not how you would do it — doesn't make it wrong.

There will be times when your members do something totally differently than you would do it — and you will need to rave about how wonderful they did.

It's time to give up being a control freak. Learn to appreciate different approaches to work. (This will be harder for some of you than others!)

As long as what your volunteer produces meets all major guidelines, use their work.

Do not redo their work.

It's disrespectful and makes volunteers mad that you wasted their time.

If your volunteer didn't follow a specific direction, the question to ask yourself is, did you remember to tell them about it?

If it's not a critical violation, run with it and become better at giving directions next time.

If it is a critical mistake, due to your omission, take responsibility and apologize immediately.

Ask the volunteer if they want you to do or help with the correction, or if they want to do it themselves.

They may have a lot of pride and ownership invested in their work — and prefer to fix it themselves.

Either way, make sure your volunteer gets proper thanks for the work they did — even if it was wrong, they still invested their time in it for you.

How you handle this will impact how willing people are to volunteer for you in the future.

11. Give directions that cover the important stuff.

- **Always cover budget, legal issues and chapter protocol when appropriate.**

You cannot hold your volunteers responsible for what you don't tell them. They are not psychic.

- **If directions are detailed, put them in writing.**

Give everyone involved a copy and go over them to make sure there are no questions.

Avoid lingo — unless everyone knows it.

- **Do not micro-manage with your directions.**

Put down as many directions as you need to and as few as you can.

You want your volunteers to be able to put their personal twist on their work to build ownership.

12. Remove ineffective key people.

Sometimes people will not be able to complete their work — and will need help stepping down from it.

This is not about being mean.

These days, a person's life can change in a moment's notice. Work gets shifted, children need help or parents get sick.

These problems can take huge amounts of time to handle — and are a higher priority than doing volunteer work for your committee.

Your key people may be committed to your cause and try to do it all — in spite of their problems.

This can do more damage than good. You need to keep on your toes to catch it as soon as possible.

A series of mini-deadlines help you to stay on top of who is keeping up with the workload.

It's easy to miss one deadline due to unexpected activities and busy schedules. As long as the person gets back on track, all is fine.

When they miss the second deadline, it's time to take some action.

Do not cop an attitude that your volunteer is lazy.

Assume instead, that something is getting in the way of their volunteer work, and they may need some help from you.

Have a private conversation with them. Explore if they need some more volunteers to work with them or perhaps a co-chair.

Give them the option of stepping down as chair and serving on the committee. Reassure them that it is fine to do and everyone will understand.

Your key person may have dreaded letting you down. This can be a wonderful gift that you give them.

If they insist that everything is back on track and they can handle it, you need to decide if you can afford to give them another chance.

If it is far out in the planning stages, let your key person continue — with the understanding that, if they need support, they need to tell you immediately and you will help find some.

If they start missing mini-deadlines again, you'll have to find them a co-chair or replacement.

If you are hitting a critical phase of the project where you don't have room for missed deadlines, share that with your key person.

Thank them for all of their effort to date, and ask them whether they would prefer a co-chair or replacement.

Keep a kind attitude and allow your friend to save face in their decision. Put yourself in their shoes.

Acknowledge what a hard decision they are making and what a true leader they are with their actions.

Hopefully with mini-deadlines and careful follow up, you won't find yourself having to take these steps.

13. How to maintain control when someone oversteps their boundaries.

You may occasionally have volunteers doing more than they are supposed to do — including making big decisions or speaking on your behalf.

Whether an overeager volunteer excited about being helpful or a past chair having a hard time letting go of control, you use the same basic approach to handle it.

- **Talk to them in private.**

You never want to discuss when your volunteer has "done wrong" in front of others. It makes you look like a bad chair.

- **Sweet - Sour - Sweet.**

This is the formula for your discussion.

Sweet: Thank them for their extra effort.

Sour: You better not cross this line again!

Sweet: I look forward to continued work with you.

Here's how it sounds for the overeager helper:

"Mary, I really appreciate how much enthusiasm and energy you are bringing to our committee.

I'm not sure if you know this or not...

When you want to double your budget for decorations, you need to talk to the committee so we can explore all of our options about where the money will come from.

We'll figure out how to deal with it this time — whether we need to take some decorations back or rearrange part of our budget.

From now on, you have to stay within the numbers you get. Okay? Great.

Sounds like you have a lot of good ideas to work with. I'm really glad you're on my committee."

It's a similar approach for the former chair...

"George, I'm glad you're helping out and sharing with me what you learned as last year's chair.

In fact, I need your help now. I need you to lay back some when I'm running our committee meetings.

For example, when we started discussing today how to promote the event, you took over the conversation and started giving everyone the answers as to how it needed to happen.

That was how you did it last year and it was great. This year, I want to explore some different options. Can you help me out by giving us the room to explore?

Great! We are truly lucky to have someone with your experience willing to be an on-call advisor."

If either person disagrees with what you ask of them, take a deep breath. Acknowledge what they say, and repeat back to them your sweet-sour-sweet statement.

For George: "George, I know you believe you ran the perfect promotion campaign last year. I hope I feel the same at the end of my year as well.

I'm very lucky to have your expertise to tap into as a foundation for what we're pursuing this year. I still need you to lay back at meetings so we can explore other options. I want to be able to use your experience to jump start our new ideas."

It may be that George is so passionate about this project that he honestly did not realize what he had done during your meeting.

If that's the case, you come up with some key phrase or signal to alert him that it's time to lay back a bit.

14. Have new and old members on committees.

New members provide fresh ideas and new perspectives. Old members provide a solid foundation to build upon.

Try and mix responsibilities from project to project.

If one person monopolizes a piece of your project year to year, you can have a disaster on your hands if they have a sudden life change and need to move or resign from your chapter.

Protect yourself. At the very least, make sure your long-timer has an educated assistant who knows what is going on with their piece of the project.

15. Make volunteering for you fun to do.

• **Appreciate your volunteers privately and publicly for everything they do for you.**

Your chapter postcards are great for this.

• **Get excited about what you are working on.**

Share that enthusiasm with your committee.

• **Encourage your members to take ownership in what you are trying to achieve.**

Think of yourself as a delegator — a facilitator of great accomplishments who is very proud of what your committee has achieved together.

Now let's go recruit those volunteers...

Chapter Eleven

How to Turn Your Members Into Active Volunteers

Recruiting volunteers to actively serve on committees and work on projects is a challenge for many.

What's missing is marketing savvy. Recruiting volunteers is simply another sale to be made.

You are selling the opportunity to volunteer in exchange for more investment of your members' time.

You need to use many of the strategies we talked about in earlier chapters on how to market your chapter to your members.

Instead of promoting a meeting, think about how those strategies could apply when you ask your members to give more of their time to volunteer. How can you hit their hot buttons better?

Here are a few more tips specific to volunteers...

12 Strategies for Getting Your Volunteers Turned On

1. Make getting involved easy to do.

• Create ways for volunteers to sign up to help outside of your meetings.

Your members may not have their calendars with them or their mind may be wandering. They may have to leave early and have not time to talk.

Put a contact names and numbers on agendas so people can call to sign up later — at their convenience.

• Repeat your request for volunteers in newsletters, flyers and on your website.

Your members are bombarded with sales pitches everyday. Multiple exposures increase the odds that members will pay attention to your request.

2. Assume your members are interested in volunteering and just need the right point of entry.

There's that old saying that you get what you expect.

The same is true with volunteers.

When you expect that your members are interested in helping, you approach recruiting them to help you in a much more positive manner.

It's not a battle of wills to get "lazy" members signed up to help out with some of the hard chapter work.

The right point of entry goes back to WIIFM — what's in it for me?

When creating volunteer opportunities, get creative in how you divide up the work. Your members have different strengths and likes.

A variety of options will hit the hot buttons of more members — and increase your work force.

3. Create easy, sound-bite opportunities.

Some people are eager to get on committees and start volunteering. Others, especially those new to your chapter, may prefer to "test the waters" first.

Help your members ease into become an active volunteer by creating easy jobs they can do with little extra effort.

Here are a few examples:

- Host a table at dinner.

- Act as a Meeting Host during social hour.

- Sit with a guest.

- Introduce the speaker.

- Help pass out materials.

- Before they leave the meeting, write a "miss you" postcard or two to members who are not there.

Your registrar or membership chair can provide them with chapter postcards and contact information.

These simple examples let your members experience what it's like to volunteer. Make sure you thank them for their help.

For some members, these sound-bite opportunities may be a perfect fit for the time they can currently give — and make them feel good about still being able to help you out.

For others, it will motivate them to take their next step in volunteering for your chapter.

4. Make it "cool" or prestigious to be involved.

People want to be part of the action.

For example, an Auto Show Benefit Night used to sell their tickets for $30 and had trouble getting minimum numbers to break even.

They raised the price to $250 and made it a prestigious event that "important" people attend. It now sells out and people clamor for tickets a year in advance.

How can you create this spin of excitement with your members and position volunteering as "the thing to do" if someone belongs?

Here's a couple of ideas...

• Talk about the great things your volunteers do both publicly and in writing.

• Have everyone who helped out that month, stand up at your meeting and applaud them.

• Use testimonials about volunteering that talk about the great connections made while helping out.

5. Create an air of excitement about being involved.

• Get dramatic with your announcements. Use skits and raps to make your point.

• Involve your current committee. Show everyone else how much fun you have as a team.

• Use trumpet music to announce a royal opportunity.

However you do it, have fun — it will make volunteering a welcomed break for members from their daily life.

6. Don't threaten your members to get involved.

This should be obvious — but, I've heard it at too many meetings to count.

"If we don't get more volunteers, we're not going to be able to pull this off. You need to sign up tonight — and take as many shifts as possible."

They hoped to motivate members to action. Perhaps a few will help. Here's what many are thinking...

"If no one else is signing up, it must not be 'the thing' to do. I'm not going to work a 'loser' project."

Or, "If I sign up, they're going to try and dump a lot of work on me. There's no way I can do it, and I don't like having to say no. I can't take that risk."

7. Don't be a martyr either!

Some people take the threat to a personal level — and assume other members care that they have personally thrown their life out of balance.

"If you don't sign up to help, Juan and I will have to do it all ourselves."

Sounds like a poorly planned project to me. They forgot to use their marketing strategies!

Your members will probably have the same responses as above to threats.

8. Recruit one-on-one during social hour.

Personally asking people to help is one of the most effective ways to recruit volunteers.

Challenge your chairs to determine how many volunteers they need for what jobs — and to work the room to fill the slots before the meeting starts.

More members may sign up when they see who else is going to help you out.

By asking in person, your chairs can tailor some opportunities to what individual members can do.

When your chairs do their reports, make sure they announce how many people already signed up — or that they got all the volunteers they needed.

Add excitement to their recruiting success. Have the new volunteers stand up and get applauded.

9. Weave member benefits and solutions into your requests for help.

Appeal to their hot buttons. What can they get out of this experience that will help them out in "real" life? Who will they help? Who will they meet?

10. Turn work into a party.

Don't have work meetings; have get-it-done parties.

Make it fun to work with you. Play music in the background. Serve food. Be upbeat about what you are accomplishing together.

11. Run good committee meetings.

• **Have an agenda.**

• **Give everyone a voice at your meetings.**

This is the time for discussion and exploring options. Make sure all of your members get a chance to give their input.

- **Be timely.**

Start and end on time. Business first, socialize later.

- **Make your meetings an experience to attend.**

My favorite committee to serve on held a meeting once a quarter. We met at the chair's home after work. She served wine, cheese, juice, special appetizers and more. Soft music played in the background.

The meeting never lasted more than 90 minutes. Attendance was usually 100%.

We felt pampered as we unwound from our day — and planned the future of our chapter.

What type of meeting experience do you provide?

12. Celebrate your successes — and give lots of thanks.

Have volunteer parties for big events. Thank your volunteers both publicly and privately.

Make your members eager to sign up to help again.

You've got your volunteers pumped up, now let's take a look at those projects for the greater good...

— Chapter Twelve —

Projects for the Greater Good

Your chapter probably has some sort of project for the greater good that you work on each term.

It may be involving students in your organization, raising funds for scholarships or contributing to other worthy causes.

This type of project not only helps a particular group of people, it also hits the hot buttons of your members who want to contribute to some greater good.

Your members will be proud to belong to your chapter due to these projects.

Projects like this may generate great media exposure in your community — and, as a result, make recruiting easier to do.

They can also drain your members' energy and create a downward spiral that's hard to break when not planned out carefully.

Let's start out by looking at fundraising...

9 Tips for Fundraising Your Members Will Love

1. Tap into your members' current skills — and the ones they want to develop.

You've heard it before and it applies here with a twist. WIIFM —What's in it for members?

You must always remember your members when planning big projects like this.

2. Maximize the return on your members' investment of their time.

Try and hit multiple hot buttons as you use your members' time.

Can they make valuable business contacts by participating? Is the committee work something they do at their convenience or socializing in a group?

3. Try different ways of raising funds.

Don't ask your members to always sell to their friends.

Here are some different ideas:

• Hold a "Pampered Pooch" contest.

• Sponsor a seminar and open it to the public.

- Help merchants hang holiday decorations.

- Put on a local talent show and charge admission.

- Hold a road rally people pay to participate in.

- Host an open networking event. Charge admission.

Get creative. There's tons of ideas out there.

4. Blow your horn.

Send out feature-based media releases. Invite reporters to attend. (See the next chapter for more ideas.)

Your members will love seeing their hard work in the local paper — even better if they're in the photo or on the news!

5. Do enough projects to achieve your goals — without burning out your members.

It may be better to do one big project with many applications than ten little ones.

The case study in the next chapter will show you how to create a big spin on one project that taps into a variety of member talents — keeping your fundraising efforts fresh and fun.

6. Keep your fundraising projects in balance with the rest of your calendar and the mission of your chapter.

Sometimes these fund-raisers grow so big that you lose sight of why people joined your chapter.

A business league got involved in bigger and bigger community service projects.

The new president liked these projects and decided to make it a goal that every member donate a couple of hours each month to a variety of causes.

This community service expectation was drilled into members at every monthly meeting. Lack of participation was frowned upon loudly.

By the end of the year, almost half of the membership left the chapter.

They had joined for business purposes. The intense focus on community service felt like a bait and switch.

7. Take care of your sponsors — especially members.

Sponsors are wonderful people and need to be thanked both personally and publicly.

Take especially good care of members who make donations to your projects.

8. Keep your fundraising projects fun.

When it becomes painful, unappreciated work, your members will find other ways to spend their time.

9. Remember why you are raising money.

Keep reminding members where the money will go and how much they are helping along the way.

One chapter calculated how many volunteer hours total — from planning to implementation — that it would take to complete their fund-raiser.

They divided that number into the amount of money they hoped to raise. Every volunteer hour worked would put them $10 closer their goal.

The chairs built a big sign to show how much "money" the chapter raised each month — multiplying total volunteer hours that month by $10.

Members got excited watching the dollars add up — and increased their volunteer efforts.

The chapter ended up raising 25% more than their original goal.

5 Deadly Fundraising Mistakes that Can Hurt Your Chapter

1. Avoid guilt tripping members to participate.

We covered this before, but it's worth bringing up again. When you make members feel bad about what they can or cannot do for your chapter, they will not come back.

Your members' time is too valuable to invest it in being involved in a group that adds to their stress and makes them feel rotten.

2. Don't make members pay to work your events.

Your members are already investing extra time in your chapter by working your event.

The food to feed volunteers is a cost of running an event — and it's less than paying regular wages.

Some groups charge their members for event T-shirts.

If members are investing their time to work your event, you need to find a way to cover their T-shirt costs in your budget.

If you have to cut your dollars so close that members need to pay to volunteer in order to make a profit, run a different project!

3. Don't alienate members with projects.

A chapter ran a golf outing and strongly requested every member to help out the day of the event.

Members who were golfers "helped out" by golfing the event — they did pay full rate.

Non-golfers were expected to work the holes, run the food events, coordinate registration — do the real work of running a golf tournament.

This "second class" worker bee status created a lot of bad feelings for the non-golfers — and the golfer members publicly proclaimed them as being silly.

As you may guess, many non-golfers quit.

Make sure your events don't alienate certain groups of members by making them feel second class.

4. Lack of volunteers means problems.

You either didn't market the value of being involved well enough or the project is not a good fit.

Your members speak volumes with the time they donate to your chapter. Listen to what it says.

Keep your members informed of fundraising projects and what help you will need as you go along.

If the lack of help is just for a certain part of the project, it may be worth hiring others to do the work.

A chapter had a directory that promoted their members to potential buyers. The board decided to upgrade the directory and needed more ad sales to cover costs.

Although the members in general loved the improved look, they did not have the time or want to sell ads.

A few members offered to sell ads in exchange for credit towards a space ad in the directory.

The board believed that the directory ads were easy to sell, and denied the trade of space for results — after all, it would set a bad precedent.

Instead, two board members acted as martyrs, and sold just enough ads to cover costs.

They got mad when other members didn't rave about the extra hours they worked to guarantee enough sales to afford the upgraded directory.

I would have agreed to the traded "commission" and opened up the opportunity to all members.

5. Avoid making every meeting "donation time" for members — whether cash, goods or services.

While fundraising is important, it's also important for your members to feel like they are getting something out of your chapter — rather than always giving.

Keep your calendar balanced with professional and personal development opportunities, social time and projects for the greater good.

It will keep your members coming back over and over.

Let's get into some details about creating enthusiasm and spin for your next project...

— Chapter Thirteen —

100+ Ways to Spin Your Projects and Build Enthusiasm — A Case Study

The Case of the Hungry Beetles

After a lot of hard work, a local chapter has raised $10,000 to give back to their community.

They learned that the pond in the middle of the community was being taking over by a nasty fungus.

The fungi created chaos in the pond and destroyed a lot of the food the fish usually eat.

The pond was quickly turning from being a place of community pride — into a real mess.

The chapter also learned a particular type of beetle could eat the fungus and clear the pond. The ecosystem would be restored and the fish would be able to live.

$10,000 was enough money to purchase the beetles needed to clean up their pond.

The members had worked hard to earn their money and were proud to be able to help their community.

They also realized by turning the beetle drop into an event, there was a bounty of opportunities to raise additional funds, promote their chapter, recruit new members, and help the community even more.

They wanted to maximize the bang for their buck — and get their members excited about being involved!

A committee was created and brainstormed over 100 different ways to create spin and enthusiasm about the chapter paying to drop those fungus-eating beetles in their pond.

Some ideas were a little crazy, and some very serious. The committee explored a variety of ways to look at the beetle drop.

Once their list was complete, the chapter had a lot of questions to answer...

- **How big did they want to make all of this?**

What did the rest of their calendar look like? How would the beetle project fit in?

- **Was this a one time shot or the start of an annual event to honor the beetles who cleaned their pond?**

- **How much volunteer power did they have?**

Did they want to do it all? Would other chapters support them? Other community groups?

- **Which spins got their members excited?**

They wanted to select spins that specific groups of members would enjoy doing or be able to explore.

This WIIFM consideration would also increase their volunteer commitment.

- **What did they want to achieve with the spin?**

New members? Community awareness? More funds for other projects? National awards? Community involvement? Outreach to young people?

Identifying the desired outcomes would make analyzing potential spins easier.

The chapter would also be able to evaluate their efforts at the end to see how the project met their goals.

It took debate and compromising for the committee to come up with answers to these questions.

The committee made a presentation to their board about their progress and got approval to move ahead.

Armed with the answer to the questions and board approval, the committee members narrowed the list to possible ideas that would meet the chapter goals.

They turned to the general membership for input.

Finally, after making sure they were on the right track, the committee put together a carefully customized package of spin activities — and truly created a project to remember.

As you read over this list, think about one of the big projects that your chapter currently runs or is planning to run during your term.

How can you add more spin to your event? What can you apply from this case study to your chapter? Let their ideas fuel your own.

The Beetle Drop Brainstorm 100+ Ideas to Add Spin To a Simple Donation

With an emphasis on Beetles...

- **Beetle parade**

- **Bug costumes contest**

- **Beetle parties to raise extra money**

    - Beetle Ball/bash/hop?
    - Can be formal/sock hop/family party?

- **Buggy bike parade**

- **VW as possible corporate sponsor?**

     - beetle car parade?
     - decorate your own beetle - cars
     - coloring contest - decorate the VW car

- **Beetles will be new citizens of the city**

     - Have a welcome party for them
     - Get the mayor to make a proclamation

- **Create a fact sheet about things you always wondered about beetles but were afraid to ask**

     - Distribute to library
     - Distribute to schools
     - Distribute to Girl Scouts/Boy Scouts/etc.
     - Distribute to media sources
     - Create informative pieces for cable TV

- **Have a poster contest for Beetle Day**

     - For children in different age groups
     - For adults for the official poster
     - Create a themed postcard(s) to use/sell
     - Hang posters in community area and vote on best with "pennies" as a fund-raiser

- Turn winners into posters or T-shirts to give away or sell

• **Have a Beetles Pride Day - everyone wear your beetle best — including our T-shirts!**

• **Have a Beetle Week of activities leading up to the big drop**

• **Buy a beetle costume**

- Have spot the beetle contests
- Have Beetle night at a local sporting event and have "Beetleman" show up

• **Sell bean bag beetles**

• **Let's eat beetle bugs!**

- Get a college professor to do a cooking demonstration on bugs you can eat
- Sell gummy bugs
- Sell suckers with bugs in them
- Have a Beetle Cake Bake Off Contest

• **Involve the Performing Arts**

- Put on a play about the Beetle Super Hero who battles the fearsome Fungi
- Get local actors involved

- Offer special Beetle Grams Service - messages from the singing beetle
- Hold a Karioke night featuring beetle/Beatles related songs
- Host a community poetry slam dedicated to our Beetle Drop
- Have a rap contest about Beetles and our drop

- **Work with schools/libraries/bookstores**

  - Collaborate for special Beetle/Beatle display
  - Have a special Beetle Book Bash
  - Identify beetle books and create bookmarks
  - Have Beetleman or Mrs. Beetle visit for special beetle storytelling
  - Book signing with an environmentalist

- **Provide lesson plan ideas for school teachers**

  - Beetle Day background and role of beetles
  - Possible activities - beetle headbands or jewelry, letter "B" sheet for little kids

- **Tie in with "A Bug's Life" movie debut — taking place next month**

  - Information booth at local theater
  - See if theater would donate % to cause
  - Be part of sneak preview night
  - Hook up with fast food promoting movie

- **Create a Beetle Speakers Bureau**

  - history of beetles or Beatles
  - beetles role in world history (like Egypt)
  - environmental issues
  - Offer programs to community groups to promote our drop day

- **Hold a writing competition for schools**

  - Get creative with topics
    - The adventures of Beetleman
    - How the beetles saved the day
    - Fables about where the beetle came from
    - Poetry about beetles
  - Have students read their stories to younger children during Beetle week
  - Create a book out of the best
    - Sell it to raise funds for school writing projects, to buy more beetles, etc.
    - Sell advertising in back of book
    - Plug your association and beetle drop day/week
  - Have special breakfast honoring budding beetle authors young and old
  - Submit stories to media for exposure
  - Create a play out of stories to be performed on drop day

Tie it to the Beatles (music group)...

- Get classic radio station to be co-sponsor of the drop
- Play Beatles music
- Have members request Beatles music and dedicate it to drop day
- Have a Beatles look alike contest
- Get Beatle impersonators to do concert

Tie to environment...

- Environmental trade show/fair
- Possible tie-in to Earth Day
- Challenge other groups to clean up part of our local community's environment
- Drop beetles on a city wide clean up day (Do we already have one? If not, suggest one)
- Team up with local environmental groups for tours of their facilities
- Nature walk to see other food chains in action.

- **Team with science teachers to do special unit relevant to Beetle Day**

    - Cleaning up environment
    - Clean water
    - Fungi (what the beetles will be eating)
    - Invasive species

• Give a science scholarship with funds raised due to beetle drop

Focus on the beetles' feast...

• Pancake feast day of drop - start eating together
• Feed the homeless day
• Hold a networking event with canned goods for homeless as admission requirement

Focus on cleaning up...

• Tour waste facility to see how the water we use in our homes is cleaned
• Sponsor a science fair for cleaning up environment
• Provide tip sheet on how to clean up anything and get out tough stains
• Have a Mr./Ms. Clean Bachelor/Bachelorette Contest - weight lifting or sell dates

• **Teach clean up skills to kids**

> - Sponsor clean up month - clean room month?
> - Have parents set cleaning goals and kids who stay clean get beetle prize
> - Create a beetle cleaning calendar.

• **Get "clean up" corporate sponsors**

> - Have appliance stores have special day and donate % of sales

- Carpet cleaners/maid services/dry cleaners-
  same types of days
- Tour cleaning aisle at store for possible large
  corporate sponsors

Using nature to help us solve our problems...

• Explore other natural solutions like penicillin
• Native American wisdom shared
• Identify other problem in community - how can
nature solve it too?

Focus on solving local challenges...

• How you can eat your problems in little steps -
simple steps that make a difference
• Create an endowment fund from proceeds to eat
other local problems
• Facilitate a problem solving day for area - invite
other groups or public

• **Sponsor a skill building workshop for community**

  - Use a local trainer, one of our members, or
    a professional speaker?
  - Relevant topics - problem solving, creative
    solutions, team building
  - Provide it free to people in need
• Write letters to your government reps challenging
them to step up to solutions

Focus on the future. Life in the pond once it is clean again...

- How to use a microscope
- Buy a microscope for local schools
- Buy a CD ROM on pond life for schools
- **Food chains explored**
    - in the pond
    - compared to humans
- **Writing contest:**
    - Stories of life under water or a city that had its sky cleared
    - How would life be different if our sky was so clouded?
- Goal setting programs
- Status reports as the beetles clear the pond

Focus within our association...

- Challenge other chapters to make a similar impact on their community
- **Write a case study about our impact**

    - Have a team speak at national convention
    - Publish success tips in national publication
    - Create a how-to manual to sell to others
    - Submit project for awards

• **Does anyone in our chapter need specific experience such as PR campaigns to get next job?**

• **Can we involve our student members?**
  - Get them credit for independent study project?
  - Ask them to manage certain parts?

• **Use to recruit new members**
  - Incorporate membership information throughout campaign
  - Call to community for extra volunteers and turn appropriate people into members
  - Set up a beetle drop hot line that includes how to become a member
  - Get corporate members at the same time as corporate sponsors
  - Invite potential members to help out

Food for Thought...

Did you get any ideas about how you can add more spin to some of your current projects?

Approaching a project this way can create a lot of fun for members — and really hit their hot buttons.

It's time to put all of the Generation Me strategies we've explored to work for you and your chapter...

Chapter Fourteen

How to Use the Ideas in This Book

Together we've covered a lot of information — from the theory behind Generation Me to specific how-to strategies to turn them into active members.

It's time to start applying them to your chapter. Here are a few tips to help you succeed.

10 Tips for Using Generation Me Strategies with Your Chapter

1. Take it one step at a time.

New thinking takes time to incorporate and adjust to.

Some of the strategies we discussed such as running a timed agenda or writing with more "You" in your copy are skills that will take practice.

Celebrate the progress you make along the way — and keep moving forward to turn Generation Me into active members of your association.

2. Apply ideas from one chapter a month.

Compare what you're currently doing to how you can add more Generation Me strategies to your mix.

3. Start with your biggest challenge.

You don't have work this book in the order it is written. Start with your biggest challenge. Work on it until you see results. Move on to the next challenge.

4. Create a support group of leaders.

Use leaders from different chapters in your association or leaders in your area from different associations.

Meet once a month to share with each other how you are addressing different Generation Me strategies.

It can be lonely being a leader. This group will be a forum for discussing strategies as well as a source of friends who understand what you're going through.

5. Get copies of this book for your board and chairs.

Have them explore strategies that apply to their areas of responsibility. Ask them to bring a report to your board meeting about how they can better reach Generation Me using some of these ideas.

There are volume discounts available on my website, www.peoplepowerunlimited.com, when you buy more than five copies.

6. Use the case study to generate more ideas for spinning your projects.

How can you apply some of the beetle drop ideas to your situation? Get a team to brainstorm together and challenge them to also come up with 100+ ideas.

7. Test different strategies.

Different strategies will work better for different chapters based on the focus of their group and the make-up of their membership.

Test strategies to discover which ones work for you.

Remember the 90-day test for board calls to remind members about meetings. You need to give the tested strategy enough time to work.

8. Share information with your members.

Knowledge is power and change can be scary — especially to older members who thought things were working great!

Share in your newsletter columns and at your meetings some of the exciting steps you're taking and the reason behind it.

Paint a picture of how this change will be a great benefit. Make sure to use WIIFM and try to hit their hot buttons as you explain what is going on.

9. Review this book quarterly.

A lot can change with your chapter in three months when you are a leader.

As you skim through the book again, you may find new information leaping out at you that wasn't relevant for you before.

10. Pass this information on to your successor.

The need for savvy marketing to Generation Me knows no time boundaries — or term limits.

Your successor will need to know the reasons and strategies to keep the efforts you started moving ahead.

As you apply these strategies, Generation Me will start to turn into active members of your association — what a great legacy to leave your chapter!

It's time for you to take your first step. Good luck!

About Cynthia D'Amour

Cynthia D'Amour, President of People Power Unlimited, specializes in helping associations create active memberships.

A certified teacher with a degree in marketing, Cynthia has more than 30 years total volunteer board experience and has recruited more than 250 members.

Cynthia was named an **1998 Outstanding Young Michigander** by the Michigan Junior Chamber of Commerce for her relationship building programs.

She's also the author of **Networking: The Skill the Schools Forgot to Teach**.

Cynthia's **R.A.R.E. Edge Leadership Series** gets association leadership pumped up with hands-on programs packed with specific, how-to solutions for them. Great for boards, chapter leadership, committee chairs, and association staff.

For more information about bring Cynthia D'Amour and the R.A.R.E. Edge to Leadership to your association, simply call, (888) 994-3375 or e-mail: damour@peoplepowerunlimited.com

For additional articles about creating an active membership for your association, check out Cynthia's website at: **www.peoplepowerunlimited.com**

Index

Symbols

A

B

C